DEDICATION

To those who hurt me and to those I may please get help because I know we all need it

ACKNOWLEDGEMENT

All thanks to God, my wife, Sarah and two lovely kids, AyoT and Bobosky.

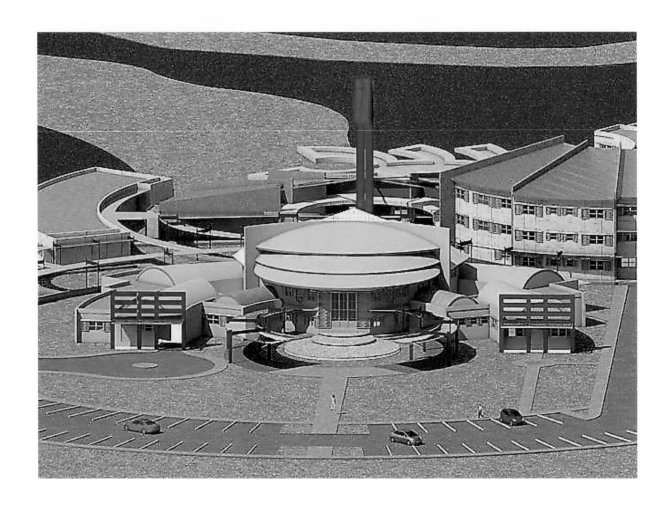

CONTENTS

PREFACE

The halfway house is a book that describes the stages of development of a young Nigerian boy in a unique way; it seeks to educate on the subject of 'objective understanding' of who we really are as 'human beings' (flawed as we are) in the simplest ways.

A summary of life that teaches both the psychology intern and the average Joe on the streets: who we are and what we are capable of doing.

This book requires a detachment from ones preconceived notion of self and others, you must act like a ghost staring at its lifeless body, critically analyzing and internalizing the issues raised in an objective manner.

Caveats though, do not engage in denial, rationalization and counter-arguments while reading this book because in the end you will lose the essence of the book; dark humor that seeks to reduce stigma associated with abnormality.

As you read, please note that the authors *Alter-Ego speech (inner voice) are in blue italics*, to give you a 3-dimensional feel of the event, *definitions are in red italics*, all other colors are hints.

DISCLAIMER

The halfway house is partly fictional and partly real, some of the events are real but the names of the actors are fictional, timelines may not be accurate and any semblances to real life accounts are co-incidental. That said, please sit-back, relax and enjoy the halfway house.

WHO AM I?

I am called the constrictor, why? Probably because of my initials, BOA *(BOA constrictor, get it?)*.

They say that a few moments after my birth, sugar ants crawled in a straight line along my body, dividing my large spherical head and tiny body into two equal halves; Mothers interpretation was that I will be extremely wealthy and famous but alas, I find that my current reality runs at odds with this flawed interpretation.

Pure African jargon some might say but only time will tell.

Every day, I wrench my fist and gnash my teeth at the unfortunate circumstance of my birth as a Nigerian, why was i born an African and even worse, a Nigerian; a country filled majorly with neurotic but oddly intelligent masses ruled by a minority of sociopathic unintelligent elitist rulers (except for a few), a blend that befuddles the mind of an average westerner.

Nigeria cannot be defined, because (as far as I know) it has no meaning and stands for nothing; what is the ideology of Nigeria besides looting, unbridled wickedness, dereliction of duty and seething lust to destroy the future of generations yet unborn?

Oh, there I go again, forgive me, I tend to lose focus, symptoms of a diagnosed depressive, from time to time, dark matter literally blinds me as I descend into the abyss.

Back to the question posed earlier, who am i?

From all said so far, you can deduce the following

1. My initials are BOA
2. I am called the constrictor (sometimes)
3. I am a Nigerian (wrenching my fist and gnashing my teeth as I wrote the 3rd point)
4. I take no pleasure in folk tales, especially the African jargon types.
5. I am a diagnosed depressive; in fact, a manic depressive.

MANIC-DEPRESSION- A bipolar disorder characterized by periods of elation (mania) which later evolves into periods of extreme moodiness (depression).

The constrictor was born in 1974 to an average Nigerian family of Yoruba extraction; life was simple in the cosmopolitan city of Lagos, father was the silent steely type, hardly showed any emotion and mother was the exact opposite, the vivacious extrovert who wore her emotions on her sleeves.

We ate rice and fried plantain only on Sundays, and Saturday mornings were for house cleaning as old school music blared loudly from fathers mechanical contraption (which had a revolving black plate) ; the term family was inclusive of grandpa, grandma, father, mother, little 'B' (my sister), aunts, uncles, cousins and the street urchins that had nowhere to lay their heads (one of the street urchins later kidnapped grandma and eloped for about 10 years).

I remember that I used to worry over how mother was increasing in size, actually thought she would explode until one day, by some strange miracle, she returned after a brief spell at the hospital with most of the weight gone, and a baby in her hands *(yet another street urchin? I wondered but alas he was introduced as my brother, little 'T', apparently he was inside mother all this time as explained by father, my thoughts went wild, she swallowed a whole person and spat him out after 9 months!)*.

I developed natural fear for mother, who wouldn't?

Mother was great though, tough but loving, a part of me feared her *(like a knight feared fire breathing dragons)* but a part of me could not do without her, a very confusing paradox. She was a hardworking, no nonsense woman, obsessed with chores and an acute compulsion to do the same thing over and over. Now that I think about it, mother was most likely plagued with obsessive compulsive disorder.

OBSESSIVE COMPULSIVE DISORDER: is an anxiety disorder in which the sufferer has persistent thought patterns (obsessions) that compels him/her to repeat certain acts routinely like rituals (compulsions).

Life was good until things changed, it was an evening like any other, mother and father were discussing in the living room and oblivious to them as usual, I was under the table getting firsthand information on the state of the nation and how our family was being affected. They brooded on how the military men in power were killing the nation with their lack of ideas and wondered how school fees would be paid among other things.

By the next day, a Saturday, mother called me and told that they had decided to change my school from a private Preparatory School on the Mainland to a public Baptist School at Surulere.

I didn't think much of this at that time but little did I know that I was about to fall faster than lightning speed (like that used to describe the devils descent) from heaven to hell. My people, believe me, if you went to public school in the late 70's/early 80's, you will know HELL IS REAL.

Day 1 in hell was a beautiful day, it started with great expectations for the new day in a new school, I was clad in my clean white shirt, shorts and socks, brand new Clark's leather shoes and my black knapsack type bag with red stripes hanging on my back *(dude was looking tight)*.

I was prancing along without a care in the world, then from the corner of my eye I noticed a couple of kids in a distance, they seemed to be hurdled together holding what seemed like a black rubber contraption pointed in my direction, new friends! (I thought), but as I turned to wave at them, there was a sudden sharp pain on my cheeks, it was so painful that I lost my balance, fell and for the first time in life, saw stars.

It felt like someone threw a rock in my face, and by the time I came back to my senses my food flask had disappeared.   The 'rock' that hit me was actually, carefully folded cardboard paper, slung from a rubber catapult the kids were holding earlier.

I eventually made it to the classroom block, the building looked like a chicken coop, it had low walls, no windows, no doors and independent metal poles holding up the roof, this was not the Private Preparatory School on the Mainland, this was HELL.

The direction of rainfall determined which side of the classroom was used and the toilets needed no introduction, nobody ever asked where the toilets were, the stench introduced them to all, far and near. My classmates were roughnecks, total jerks, some of whom wore no shoes to school *(who were those people? No shoes!)*.

Needless to say that I was easy pickings and was bullied regularly but they were magnanimous some times and allowed me take one spoonful of food from my packed lunch.

The bullying continued for a long time until father told me to stand up for myself one day when mother wasn't looking, "give them hell", he said *(well, maybe not in those exact words but that's what I heard)*, so I ensured the food ended up on the bully's head for the next few days and I still remember the beatings that followed that bravado *(one teardrop just fell from my eye as I typed that)*.

Father was right though, because not only did the bullying stop, they actually showed me respect, I earned my stripes through blood and sweat, I was now officially one of the roughnecks and my fame grew

(Ode after ode was sung to my courage and bravado, that's my story and I am sticking to it).

Those roughnecks exhibited symptoms associated with Anti-Social Personality Disorder.

ANTI-SOCIAL PERSONALITY DISORDER is a disorder in which the sufferer exhibits a pattern of criminal, impulsive, callous and ruthless behavior, with utter disregard for the rights & feelings of others and disrespect for rules of defined social norms.

Some of those kids saw their fathers beat their mothers to points of coma, men in motor parks where they worked after school raped young female hawkers; hard drugs were used in public spaces among many other vices without repercussion.

Like I said earlier, HELL IS REAL.

At some point, I was transferred from school 3, hitherto referred to as HELL, to school 2 (HADES) which was still within the same school confines, school 2 had story buildings, with doors and some windows here and there, toilets still needed no introductions, but life was somewhat better, the roughnecks here wore shoes but kept their distance because my fame preceded me *(remember the Ode's?)*.

Here I was king, people talked in hushed tones around me as I strutted my stuff (in my mind, I heard them say "there goes the famed constrictor", I later learnt they were saying "there goes the dude who brings Eba and Okro soup to school for lunch"), it didn't matter though, here, I was king, prancing around like MOFASA, the lion king until one day, Mrs. O-Dung (our class teacher) introduced a new student to the class.

The class captain shouts out loud: *"All stand (we all stood, that's the ritual), greet (we sang, good mooooorning ma, God bless you, also a ritual)".*

Mrs. O-Dung: *"Class meet Juliet, she will be joining us from now on, what do you say to Juliet class".*

Class: *"Hello Juliet, you are welcome to primary 5 so and so, God bless you" we sang.*

Everybody sat, except me, as I followed Juliet's movement with my eyes as she proceeded to her seat, drooling like the village idiot *(who was this angel in human form that had come to abide with us in HADES, I pondered)*. The crack of Mrs. O-Dungs cane on my desk brought me back to life and I sat, everyone laughed.

From that moment, Juliet (Julie baby as I fondly called her in my daydreams) dominated my sub-conscious realm, whenever she asked me a question *(rarely)*, my mouth opened to speak but words never came out, my friends said I often coughed and spoke in strange tongues but I could have sworn they were lying, because my words were clear (to me at least) as I confessed my undying love to Juliet *(Julie baby)*.

I was the person appointed to write down the names of noise makers whenever Mrs. O-Dung left the classroom but for some strange reason, chatter box Juliet *(Julie baby)* never made the list *(what a wooose)*, then one day, Fausat made the list, Fausat was a huge MAN-GIRL, she looked like a man *(had facial hair too)*, but we were told she was a girl, Fausat was a Togolese house help by night and pupil by day, Fausat had rippling muscles, Fausat was twice my size. Everyone feared Fausat.

On this fateful day, Fausat made Juliet *(Julie baby)* cry earlier in the day and had become marked in her eyes, so as soon as Fausat whispered, Juliet *(Julie baby)* shouted to me that Fausat spoke and asked if I was going to ignore this wrong.

I broke out in cold sweat and started to stammer, but Juliet *(Julie baby)* called my name in an assuring way and whispered softly in my ear, "constrictor dear, be strong for me" (true story), and to cut a long story short, Fausat made the list *(another teardrop just fell from my eye)*.

Fausat (man-girl & twice my size) ran to my desk, huffing and puffing (like the wolf in three little pigs story) as she demanded that her name be erased immediately, Juliet *(Julie baby)* held my arm and said "constrictor darling, do the right thing" *(that's what I heard)*, so I stood up like Winston Churchill and said in a puritan voice, "Fausat, you are on the list, and that's final".

Before the statement ended, Fausat was on me like white on rice, she pummeled me good. The class went wild, with all the boys rooting for me while all the girls (except Julie baby) were for Fausat, oh, she beat me but by some stroke of luck, she fell and her back became exposed, with all the strength I could muster, I gave her a full double open-palms whammy on her back, Fausat shrieked in pain and started to cry, I was declared the undisputed winner by the boys as they carried me shoulder high chanting war songs.

After a few seconds, the pain from the blows Fausat inflicted on me started to take effect, tears welled up in my eyes and the boys quickly wiped them before the girls could see, whispering to me "no spoil man" *(which meant that I shouldn't disgrace men, as MEN DON'T CRY)*. Yes, that ever present stereotype that cuts across cultures, MEN DON'T CRY, we bottle up the pain.

After Mrs. O-Dung returned, Fausat and I made the toilet washing list as punishment for the altercation that occurred earlier. The things we do for love, Surely Juliet *(Julie baby)* would see me as her hero or so I thought, sadly the reverse was the case, she crushed me by calling me "toilet boy", and she rebuked me for calling her name, how could she, who was worshipped from school 1 to 3 be my friend *(school 1 to 3, really? She was a newbie hardly known in school 2).*

"Know thy place, toilet boy" was what she said to me, those words cut like a knife, I felt little and used, Juliet was a Narcissist.

NARCISSISTIC PERSONALITY DISORDER: is a disorder in which the sufferer has grandiose thoughts of self-worth, with disregard for other people's feelings and often seeks to exploit others; as they see themselves as being superior to others.

Guess who made number 1 on the noise makers list the following day? (Smiley face).

AN UNFAIR WORLD

1983 was the year my parents made me sit for the national common entrance examinations, this was the entrance exams we took to gain admission into the Federal Government owned schools (popularly referred to as Unity Schools, as they were intended to further unify the country since children from different parts of the country attended),

Grandma was very happy and expectant, especially since she was a proud alumnus of a Unity School herself, Queens College, Yaba, the best unity school for girls at that time. She boasted to her friends that I would be attending the male version, Kings College soon, this was clearly a big deal in my family and much was expected of me.

You see, I come from a fairly cerebral lineage, maternal grandma was a retired Chief Matron of a General Hospital, both grandpas were Permanent Secretaries of the defunct Western Regional Government , father was a practicing engineer, mother was a personnel manager, aunts and uncles were a mix of different professional occupations, it's like I said, a fairly cerebral lineage.

Unfortunately, by the time my results came, I was told I could not gain entrance into Kings College even though I passed, it turned out that the geographical location of birth determined cut off mark, southerners had higher cut off marks because northerners were considered to be educationally disadvantaged, the implication of this was that northerners who got much lower scores would be granted admission.

I remember the anger and frustration I felt as I looked to my parents for answers but sadly they had none; it's an unfair world.

Mother, the ever optimistic extrovert cut into my dark moment and assured me that there were other great schools, looking at dad and the education board member we were conversing with for support, they quickly nodded in agreement somewhat halfheartedly, but I could sense the pessimism in the air.

Mother rationalized that she preferred schools far away from home anyway and would not have approved even if I made the cut, "go out there" she said, "see the world beyond Lagos" she said. My mood brightened, it would be fun to see beyond Lagos, or so I thought.

Thus my adventure began, Federal Government College Ugwuolawo, would be my next port of call. Ugwuolawo, was situated in the middle belt region of Nigeria until it was ceded to Kogi state (a new state carved out of Kwara, Niger and Benue states).

My parents had never been there and it was fun to watch them argue all through the journey, father insisted on using his trusty map while mother thought it was best to ask for directions from the locals along the way, it was typical *(I love those guys)*. We got to a town called Agene-Bode in the defunct Bendel state(now Edo state), where we were told that we had missed the ferry that would transport us to Idah, the town before Ugwuolawo, so we ditched our car and boarded an improvised canoe with a boat engine and rudder attached.

It was all fun and games until we got to the middle of the river when the engine suddenly stuttered and stopped, with no land anywhere in sight, the captain *(funny, he said captain)* of the canoe asked us not to panic, my 9 plus years flashed before my very eyes as he tugged forcefully at the engine rope, miraculously, the make-shift rickety boat purred back to life and we completed the journey to Idah.

Benue people were strange, they spent a lot of time greeting each person along their paths such that you wondered how they eventually made it to work, each course of greeting lasted about 5 minutes; they would often stoop low as though they wanted to bump shoulders, touched their chests and repeated words over and over.

After about 8 hours on the road, we finally made it to Ugwuolawo and my parents left for Agene-Bode immediately, as I settled in it suddenly felt alone, here I was in a strange place with strange people all around me, scared, alone and with number 2 beckoning (which was slang for poop time), so I asked a young gentleman, Senior Arrogant Peacock, for the loo, in perfect queen's English *(he was trying to show off)*, Senior Arrogant Peacock asked another fellow, in perfect pidgin English, "Wetin be loo?" *(Which means what is a loo?)*, other fellow replies "e be like say na toilet" *(which means I think it is toilet)*, Senior Arrogant Peacock smiles mischievously and exclaims "ha, ok, loo! Follow me".

I followed and we went out of the room, walked for about 2 minutes, entered a bush path, walked for another 2 minutes until we came to a ramshackle shed with wooden frames, covered top and sides with zinc roofing material, I suddenly recognized the smell from a not too distant past, with flies bigger than bees threatening our slow but deliberate approach, the buzzing intensified to warn us that we were encroaching on their territory.

Senior Arrogant Peacock suddenly stops dead in his tracks, turns to me and said "LOO!" pointing at the shed, *(we really hated that guy)* I summoned courage and opened the make shift door, what I saw haunted me for days to come, I saw excreta splattered round a hole, with huge maggots doing the Tango all over the floor. Number 2 quickly disappeared as I bolted back to the dormitory; I still hear the laughter of arrogant peacock till this day. If I thought school 3 was hell, I was sadly mistaken, this was HELL raised to the power of 2.

I slowly adapted to hell part 2 and life was getting better, never mind the bullies, mosquitoes, rats that gnawed our feet at night while we slept, and snakes we sometimes found in our beds, life was getting better.

The worst moment came when I took ill and was taken to the sick bay, one of the upper six students; a known BRUTISH BULLY came to visit his younger brother who was also admitted in the sick bay, as I slept, I suddenly heard someone push aside my separating curtain *(he was a light sleeper)*, senior brutish bully tip-toed to the side of my bed and started unzipping my pants, I laid there pretending to be in deep sleep, too scared to shout.

He finally succeeded in unzipping me and grabbed Mr. JT *(my personal slang for penis),* before he could do anything further, the nurse on duty made a sound outside and he bolted out of the place leaving my fly hanging out of my unzipped pants, I had never experienced anything like this as I was a protected child who hadn't even learnt about the full details of heterosexual relationships talk less of homosexuality, confusion cannot adequately describe what I felt at that time.

Senior brutish bully was a pedophile.

PEDOPHILIA: is a sexual dysfunction where an adult attempts or desires sexual gratification by engaging in sexual activities with young/underage children.

Needless to say that I avoided this particular senior like a plague in the following days, couldn't even make eye contact with him when our paths crossed, after a period of our cat and mouse charade, I reckon that he figured I knew what had happened and he picked on me at every possible turn.

He would come looking for me (even though our rooms were far apart) to go fetch water or engage in one chore or the other, things got to a head one day when I stood up to him and told him my parents did not send me to school to fetch water; he became enraged and kicked me in the groin *(it hurt really bad).*

The school authorities took me to the hospital after a couple of days in the school clinic without any respite from the pain, it was a teaching hospital in Benin city, the constrictor had developed Torsion.

TORSION: is a medical term that describes the entanglement of the chord (vas deferens) that connects the testicles (inside the scrotum) to the penis (via the prostate gland).

Only a surgical procedure could correct this ailment, and I remember hearing the doctor tell my parents it could lead to infertility in future if it wasn't corrected quickly.

It really is an unfair world.

GRANDMA GOES MISSING.

After the "Torsion" incidence, my parents felt they had more than they could stomach from Ugwuolawo and organized for my transfer to yet another unity school closer to home *(closer? Dude, it was 4 hours from home)*, Federal Government College Ogbomoso was the school where I resumed my second year of secondary education. Gladly, there was no river crossing on this journey and it lasted about half the time it took to get to the other school.

The year was 1985 and there was uncertainty in the air, General Mohammed Buhari was just toppled as Head of State and replaced by General Ibrahim Badamosi Babangida (popularly referred to as IBB at the time), my parents were strangely quiet all through this trip, depression filled the air, because someone had kidnapped Grandma.

My maternal grandma was a strict disciplinarian, stiff and showed very little emotions, she and grandpa had separated for many years before I was born and it was my opinion that this was the reason for her stiff awkward nature.

She had 2 biological and many adopted children, mother was first and uncle LOVE second, even as children, we could tell that mother was grandpa's favourite while uncle love was grandma's; grandpa had other children from other women though, as a socialite he was wealthy and quite popular, but sadly I remember very little of him because he died shortly after I turned 7 years.

I remember grandma and mother argued regularly, they were like cat and dog those 2, grandma disapproved of mothers love for street urchins and definitely didn't want to house some pregnant white garment person from off the streets but mother prevailed on her citing compassionate reasons *(this is not a discriminatory remark towards white garment churches and should not be regarded as such)*.

This would be the greatest error my mother ever made, a decision that rocked the very foundation she stood on, which was built around love and trust.

Within a few years of co-habitation with grandma, the street urchin in question kidnapped grandma and disappeared, she simply varnished and the police could not find them, from time to time the urchin would appear and disappear like a ghost, and one or two properties belonging to grandma would change ownership.

This incidence put a lot of strain on mother and her siblings, their relationships became cold and less cordial, one of my uncles could not keep a steady relationship with the opposite sex for long, he divorced his wife, had children from another and dated a couple more, he became overtly dramatic and temperamental, he developed what psychologists refer to as Histrionic Personality Disorder.

HISTRIONIC PERSONALITY DISORDER: is a disorder characterized by quick change in moods, unstable relationships with an intense need for attention and approval.

Mother on the other hand developed one of the Anxious-Fearful personality disorders. She was never the same again.

ANXIOUS-FEARFUL PERSONALITY DISORDER: is characterized byt a chronic sense of anxiety and fearfulness, and behaviors intended to ward off feared situations.

Now, where was i? *(Ogbomoso)* **yeah, thanks** *(you are welcome)*, **back to the Ogbomoso journey.**

Ogbomoso seemed better than Ugwuolawo at first glance, for one, the senior and junior dormitories were separated from one another, which meant there was less bullying, the pit latrine and open bathing area were just behind the hostel and it was generally more sanitary than what I was used to *(even though people still excreted on newspapers in different areas of the latrine).*

I was finally living the life or so I thought, until one fateful day, the senior student in charge of our dormitory woke us up in the dead of the night, told us to line up in straight lines according to our room numbers *(like we did every morning for morning devotion)*, **the fellow was a huge muscular MAN** *(in my mind's eye he was about 30'ish)* **and was known for his aggressive and violent conduct.**

His husky voice boomed into the silent night sky as he accused some of us of being wizards, who turned into

mosquitoes at night to torment him *(true story, I swear)*, we all laughed, thinking it was some kind of cruel twisted joke*(he even jokingly asked some of his pals where the hidden cameras were hidden)*, "SHUT UP" he bellowed like a military drill sergeant *(turns out dude was dead serious)*, he then called out a few students and marched them to the back of the hostel for "interrogation". By the time they returned, most were badly hurt, some even confessed to the charge of wizardry to escape the beating.

He lined the newly confessed wizards before us and promised to fish out the remaining wizards amongst us in good time *(fear suddenly enveloped my young heart again)*, he even set up a wizard hunting task force *(I kid you not)*, and this was how HELL part 3 began.

Senior WIZARD HUNTER made good on his threat as he hunted for the wizards every night, looking for whom hardly slept at night or who slept in weird positions; God was gracious to me and I never got into his categorization criteria until he got a dream that the short ones were the chief wizards *(I peed my pants)*. Senior Wizard Hunter invited me to join him at the back of the hostel for interrogation at dusk and I knew that was the end.

Back then, we had no mobile phones and there were only 3 telephones in the entire school, one in the principal's office while the other 2 were in the vice-principals' office; the only way to contact home was either via post or telegram at the postal office which was about an hour's walk to town after a rigorous application process to get a permit to visit town.

The die was cast, this was not a David versus Goliath moment, it was more like a mini-David versus 2XGoliath moment and no magic stone from a sling could solve this problem; as night approached I understood firsthand what the bible meant when it described the size of the drops of sweat falling from the saviors face.

Darkness suddenly enveloped the sky and we were summoned to the back, he took on the bigger kids first, knocking them to the ground over and over like light weight bags with his fist, they begged for mercy but he didn't stop until they confessed.

Then he finally called me, the last wimp standing, he looked into my eyes for a bit breathing out hot air like a Spanish arena bull *(I peed my pants again, damn that bladder)*, he shook his head and by some miracle asked me to go without laying a finger on me.

I cried all the way to my room, *(I think it was the trauma or maybe I just didn't want the others to feel alone in their pain)*, after this traumatic experience, I slept with one eye open and discovered that I had regressed such that I started bedwetting again.

This continued for almost a year, and to stop this, I would tie Mr. JT with a rope so the pain of the force of fluid could wake me. I was showing some signs of Post-Traumatic Stress Disorder (PTSD).

POST TRAUMATIC STRESS DISORDER: is an anxiety disorder characterized by repeated dreams of a traumatic experience, heightened state of arousal and associated detachment from social situations.

Senior Wizard Hunter was a Paranoid Schizophrenic.

PARANOID SCHIZOPHRENIA: is a disorder characterized by delusions of grandeur and hallucinations involving themes of persecution and grandiosity.

He believed an entire hostel of students were wizards who hated him so much (delusions of grandeur) that they reverse-evolved into mosquitoes just to torment only him every night (hallucinations of persecution).

There were a few bricks missing from his building.

By the time I got promoted to the senior hostel, things took a turn for the worse, senior students tormented our lives at every turn, you could not survive the day without fetching a minimum of 5 buckets of water, washing dirty clothes and collecting food on their behalf from the dining hall.

At the end of the day we were usually too tired to study and slept during prep time (this was a period when we were expected to study, shortly after dinner and before lights out); as soon as we returned from prep, the senior students would allow us sleep for a couple of hours, before dragging us out of our beds violently, beating us as they ushered us to the center of the hostel.

They would ask us to lie down on the bare red earth and step on our backs to cross from one corridor to the other because their royal feet was not meant to touch red earth, I also remember one time when one of them poured urine on us as we lay helpless on the ground.

They would force us to lie down on the bare red earth and step on our backs to cross from one corridor to the other because their royal feet was not meant to touch red earth, I also remember one time when one of them poured urine on us as we lay helpless on the ground.

As if that was not enough, they would then tell us to engage in difficult military type exercises as punishment for trumped up charges of leaving the hostel dirty. Operation "WARA-WORO" as it was fondly called by our seniors at the time was pure evil and we had little or no protection from the school authorities, in fact I remember that whenever we reported, the teachers simply told us it was SCHOOL LIFE and consoled us that our turn to persecute others would eventually come when we became seniors.

This was a very difficult period in my life, How did this happen? Why was everything so hard? Who moved my cheese? *(Ok, maybe the last question is a little made up, but you get the gist)*. I remember one time, when my father brought me back to school after midterm holiday at home and I suddenly broke down in tears begging him to take me out of the jungle *(in fairness to father, he was never told the bitter tales of woe)*, his response was classic, it would remain in my subconscious from that day on, "come on son, be a man", I had forgotten, MEN DON'T CRY.

I BECAME A MAN THAT DAY, my problems were mine and mine alone to solve, nobody cares, nobody will come to save you; and then the voices began, audible voices that asked me to end it from time to time.

The first time I heard the voice, I thought I was losing my mind but then, maybe I was, it was in the chemistry laboratory, teacher CAMEO was teaching on acids and alkaline and the voice asked me to drink one of the labeled acidic substances, it was feminine and seductive but I didn't drink it *(duh! Obviously).*

Suicidal Ideation began and I could hear voices other people did not hear *(Dude, you realize I can hear you, right?)*, they finally broke the constrictor.

SUICIDAL IDEATION: a process in which one's mind becomes pre-occupied with thoughts on if, when or how to take one's life.

THE HALF-WAY HOUSE

Some of my friends and I became "travellers", the term used to describe us because we lived our lives on the road *(like nomads)* to escape the suffering in the hostel; we bought mini-travelling bags, loaded them with bare essentials (uniforms, toiletries, slippers/shoe etc.) and hit the road, where we found ourselves at night was where we lay our heads, sometimes we slept in the classrooms, at other times on trees.

My friends were great though, NOHO the great, ABATI the Hun, the man from WALES, O-HAIRY, man JADI, LOMZY short stuff, skinny SAO, RABBIT, O-MIKS, to mention a few, they were the only source of joy Ogbomoso had to offer, it was sad to part ways but nothing lasts forever. We graduated from Ogbomoso eventually *(good riddance)*.

At some point, after my graduation from secondary school, grandma was found eventually.

The urchin brought her to Lagos (from the North) to finalize a business transaction that required her physical presence, unfortunately for the urchin, someone who worked in the hotel where they lodged recognized them and quickly informed mother.

Grandma was brought home in a drugged state, she had no recollection of who she was nor whom we were, it took about a week before she regained some of her senses and as time passed she became majorly depressed when she realized what was lost. She became delusional and hallucinated often, grandma lost her mind.

MAJOR DEPRESSION: is characterized by extreme moodiness, often accompanied with weight loss or decreased appetite, inability to sleep or the reverse (sleeping for too long), feelings of tiredness, worthlessness (which can lead to suicidal ideation or suicide).

When it became obvious to my parents that this was beyond home care *(duh!)*, they got her admitted to the psychiatric hospital on the LEFT, but mother could not bear the stigma of our family name being marred by tales of insanity, so she got her discharged against doctors' advice and made private arrangements for psychiatric care at home.

I could not understand the rationale behind this decision, dad and mum weren't rich, but they preferred to part with a pretty sum just to avoid shame, these were the same people who taught me to live my life without fear of peer influence, it was intriguing but my interest in psychiatry and psychology increased with every visit by the good doctor A-Gun.

While all these happened, I gained admission into the University of Lagos *(pure luck)*.

I passed the JAMB exam (Joint Admissions Matriculation Board examination) *(barely)* but my score was actually far below the cut off mark *(no thanks to the Quota System again)*, so it was decided that I would sit for the exam the following year, it didn't bother me much as I had come to believe nothing good ever happened to me anyway; while I prepared my mind, mother suddenly barged into my room *(this was a habit, the barging)*, she and father met a man, she then proceeded to describe the lovely canopies, the ambience of the party, how her outfit was the best at the party, and oh, don't get her started on the food *(this too was a habit, the loss of focus)* but before she could continue, I interrupted her saying "Mother, you met a man?".

She slapped my head somewhat playfully *(it actually hurt, she was wearing large gold rings)*, "don't interrupt your mother dear", she said, "yeah, so where was I?" I replied "you met a man" and moved two steps back in case she decided to be playful again.

Yes, she met a man, WISE OLD OWL; he was the big shot at the department of architecture at that time, by some uncanny coincidence he sat next to them at the party and as they made conversation, he introduced himself, mother said she was besides herself and proceeded to tell me of how she knew the day was going to be a lucky day, she actually saw her long dead father in a dream, he was smiling at her and to top it all, her palms itched, her palms never itch unless God was planning something, blah blah blah blah *(I knew it was going to be a long evening)*.

The WISE OLD OWL said he would like to meet with me and so they took me to him, he had fluffy white hair, his eyes pierced right through you like they could see your thoughts *(yes, I felt so naked, creepy stuff)* and you could tell that he was an erudite scholar; He asked me a few questions and for some odd reason, the chair I sat on seemed to get warmer by the minute. The WISE OLD OWL decided to put me on his discretionary list and that's how I became an architecture student. Thank you WISE OLD OWL.

Architecture was tough, the lecturers grilled us and we were always having multiple deadlines every week, there was GERMAN machine (*dude actually spoke German*), the ASSASIN (*always wore a trench coat & dark glasses in the tropics, must have spent a fortune on deodorants*), mother superior O-BEM, missisi B-ANJ (*missisi was how she pronounced Mrs., true story*), the GAP toothed maverick (*dude talked to himself often, we liked him, yes we did*), DAODA the sexy guy (*hardly, he was short, not like me though, much shorter, he had a big tummy, well, bigger than mine and he drooled at the sight of beautiful women, why am I sensing a pattern here?*), crafty WIG, hippie E-SAN, to name a few.

My journey through the University was not without its problems though, there were multiple strike actions embarked upon by lecturers, riots by students that often led to the closure of the school by the authorities and rival cult clashes that usually led to some persons death.

I remember a particular clash that happened one fine evening when I was in my friend's room, gun shots suddenly filled the air and D-TAL (my best friend) killed the lights, while I took a defensive posture (*defensive posture? we were under the bed, trembling and saying our last prayers*) **when I remembered D-TAL had mentioned that his neighbor was actually a cult don, "what if the rival cult group members head this way?", I thought to myself.**

It became obvious that we were sitting ducks, so I summoned courage, bolted out of the door and made a dash for the stairs.

I made it to the ground floor, and cautiously moved towards my car, a Mercedes Benz 200, but before I could open the door, I heard someone groaning in pain in the drain, the fellow was badly hurt, covered in his own pool of blood with machete cuts all over his head and body, I looked around and saw another fellow hiding in another drain, luckily he was unhurt and I beckoned on him to come help the injured student.

As we started moving him, one of the cultists looked back (apparently they hadn't gone too far) and made a mad dash for us, luckily we were able to drive off with him before he got to us. I had never driven so fast in my life and my heart was racing, the fellow who assisted in moving the injured person was actually a fellow architecture student (I did not recognize him early due to the panic) and together we rushed him into the emergency unit at the school health center.

The clinic was overwhelmed with many casualties, and the doctors were not happy to see us but they couldn't turn us back, so they asked us to put him on a trolley and wait in the reception area,. We obeyed without question; there was no need to add to their stress besides how would we be of assistance in the emergency room.

While waiting, my colleague suddenly pinched me and suggested that we disappear before we got accused of being his assailants, I didn't argue and we craftily disappeared as the doctors battled to save his life, it was a great relief to hear that the fellow survived the following day but I never bothered to find out who he was, I didn't want any problems.

The roughnecks from primary school days had evolved into psychopathic serial killers.

These psychopaths had no feelings for the lives they destroyed, they saw their victims as mere objects, like lifeless pawns that could be sacrificed, and they felt nothing.

The more I studied my environment closely through the prism of psychology, I discovered that we all exhibited some form of abnormality; some had it worse than others but often chose to live in denial.

We had blood thirsty psychopaths in cult groups maiming and killing fellow students, nymphomaniac lecturers sexually harassing and raping students, suicidal students taking their lives, abnormal behavior festered unchecked, yet we buried our heads in the sand like ostriches hoping that the predator will not see us because we had chosen not to see it but it didn't go away, instead it graduated and has taken over reins of government.

PSYCHOPATHY: is characterized by lack of remorse and empathy, little or no emotion and utmost disregard for the lives of other people.

It has permeated every fabric of our society; it's in the bus we ride daily, at our offices and in our homes. This is our shared reality, the abnormal has finally become the norm, with this at the back of my mind, I decided to design a place that could alter this reality as my final year thesis project; I called it THE HALF-WAY HOUSE.

The halfway house was my happy place, the place where stigma was none existent, the place where i could seek help and not be ashamed, and the place where every day folk gathered from time to time to watch the sunset at the beach front while receiving much needed professional psychological help.

The HALF-WAY HOUSE is my place of healing even though it's in my head.

So, if man is said to be a by-product of his environment, then we all need to define who we are based on this premise, we all need to ask ourselves that deep soul searching question, WHO AM I?

This is the question i hope to find answers to some day,

But while I await answers, one thing is certain,

I accept that I am Abnormal but not Insane.

#STOPTHESTIGMA

All psychology definitions are adapted from the following reference -

Nolen-Hoeksema, S. (1998). Abnormal Psychology. McGraw Hill: Boston, Massachusetts.

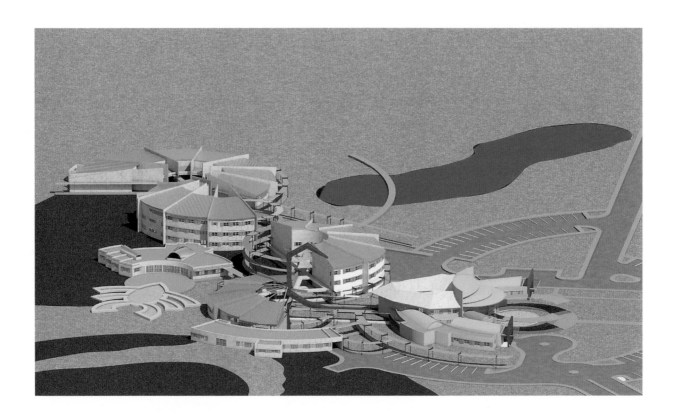

Printed in Great Britain
by Amazon